by Erica

365

Daily Inspirations & Quotes
for the fascinating teen girl

365

Daily Inspirations & Quotes

for the fascinating teen girl

by Erica Mills-Hollis

legacy . love . tradition

Precious Heart Publishing, LLC
6841 Virginia Parkway
Suite 103, #218
McKinney, TX 75071

www.apreciousheart.com

Phone: 800-387-4851

Published by: Precious Hearts Publishing, LLC

Daily Inspirations & Quotes
For the Fascinating teen girl

ISBN: 978-0-98593970-0

Library of Congress Control Number: 2012913621

Printed in the United States of America

Dedication

This book is dedicated to every teen girl all over the globe. In this world you may face many adversities and obstacles, and my job is to keep you inspired and motivated so that you can conquer all your dreams and aspirations 365 days a year. Happy Reading!!!

January

January 1

As you embark on this new journey that we call a new year; embrace this new beginning with a clean slate. Remove any and everything in your life that doesn't belong there. All fear, negativity, and discouragement must go and replace it with faith, hope, and as many dreams as you can dream. This is a new you. Last year's you was cool, but this year's you is awesome. Nothing and no one will stand in the way of your dreams, because you are on the move.

Happy New YOU to you!!!!

January 2

As you walk out your front door today and feel the cold winter chill all the way to the bone that makes you shiver and wakes up every vital organ within you; this is a miraculous sign that you are alive. And being alive gives you the opportunity to be creative and spread your magical chills all over the world so that you can be able to reach someone else within. What shivers will you send today?

January 3

"Sticks and stones may break my bones, but words will never hurt me." Somebody lied, because words do hurt. But it's important to remember that you are not who they say you are. You are so much more. You are a leader, and an encourager. So hold your head up high. God created you, uniquely and you should be proud about it. If anyone has a problem with who you are, tell them to take it up with God.

January 4

"Sugar, spice, and everything nice." Sugar; stay sweet. Don't let life's hardships turn you bitter. You have too much going for yourself, whether you know it or not. Protecting your innocence is the key. Spice; although you are sweet, you must possess a little spice so that no one can run over you. You have to let your peers know what you will not put up with. If they have a problem with it, it's time for new friends. You need motivators not hesitators. Everything nice; don't be afraid to lend a helping hand. The one person that you go the extra mile for could one day be the person who goes five extra miles for you. You never know who can be a blessing to you one day. Treat everyone like you want to be treated.

January 5

When you look into the mirror, what do you see? I hope that you see beauty. No matter your height, race, size, hair type, or clothes. You are a beautiful young lady who is going to blossom into a beautiful woman. But more importantly, I hope that you also see inner beauty; it by far out ways the outer beauty. If you are beautiful inside, you can't help be beautiful outside. Take a picture and smile big, because you are beautiful.

January 6

Today is, *"do something nice day."* Why not pick up an extra chore for the day. Or maybe help your teacher pass out papers. Help a friend carry her books if your hands are free. Whatever it may be, just make sure it's from the heart. If you feel put out by it, I don't want you to do it. I'm just trying to help you set the foundation for the type of woman you are going to be. Being nice doesn't cost a thing.

January 7

Roses are red, violets are blue, I have so much faith in you and you should too. I know it's not always easy being a girl. We are very emotional people and are easy to get our feelings hurt. But being a girl has its perks. We love unconditionally, we have a soft hand that can calm the world if need be, and we are just fabulous creatures. Simply put; we rock. So embrace your femininity, because girls rule.

January 8

On those days when it feels so hard to get out of bed in the morning, remember there is light at the end of the tunnel. You may feel the pressures of school and acceptance weighing heavy on your shoulders, but you have to get up. How will you conquer your dreams if you don't ever get up? Everyone has those moments, so don't get me wrong, but you can't stay there. Pick yourself up and hit the ground running. I promise it will pay off in the end.

January 9

What do you want to be when you grow up? That is a question that you are asked from the day you are probably capable of saying a complete sentence. But the pressure really starts once you enter high school. Don't worry; if you're still at the point in your life where you don't know what that dream job is, you still have a little time left. But I suggest you use it wisely. Just ask yourself *"what do I love doing, and if someone offered me a million dollars to do want I love, what would it be?"* Also think about any special skills that you may have. God has already equipped you with special gifts and skills so that you will successfully be able to carry out his plan for you.

January 10

In this life you will make mistakes, but you are much bigger than your mistake. A mistake is just a learning tool of how not to do things. So the next time you will be more than capable of doing it the right way.

January 11

Did you pray last night? If so what did you pray for? Remember God always hears your prayers. Just trust and believe and he will come through for you.

January 12

Smile. It takes fewer muscles to smile than it does to frown. Don't over work yourself if you don't have to. Besides, you're way cuter when you smile. ;-)

January 13

Hey pretty girl. Yes you. Don't you know how pretty you are? If you don't, now you do. And no one can tell you differently. Except that fact that you are just gorgeous. Just don't let it go to your head.

January 14

A thousand shall fall at thy side, and ten thousand at thy right hand; but it shall not come nigh thee. *Psalms 91:7:* You see God has your back; He won't let nothing or no one hurt you. Girl you're protected.

January 15

Today is *"Say Something Hat Day."* Wear a hat that expresses your uniqueness and creativity. You are outside the box, so let it speak boldly of you. Whether it's a Fedora, cowgirl brim, or a baseball cap; wear it well.

January 16

When you choose a role model, make sure she is someone that is honest, has high morals, and represents the true meaning of womanhood. She must be a lady that embodies every aspect of the word *"lady."* I don't want you to be lead astray.

January 17

A leader is someone who sets the standard for themselves, not caring if they fit in with society's limits that are now called popular. A follower is someone who wants to fit into the society of popular no matter how detrimental the crowd. Be a leader.

January 18

Organization is a helpful tool to carry through life. Today organize your thoughts, school work, and your room; then you'll be able to organize your home, work, and family. No need for cluttered chaos.

January 19

Studying is preparation for success. How can you be successful at something if you know nothing about it?

January 20

Being a teenager can be very hard, but continue to do what you have to do now, so that one day you can do what you want to do later.

January 21

When everything around you seems like it's falling apart; I want you to find comfort in knowing that you have a roof over your head, or maybe that you were able to eat a hot meal last night. There is someone out there that is worse off than you will ever be.

January 22

Today is a great day for you to start saving money. If you can save $5 a week; in four years you will have $1,040. If you can't start out with $5, try $2 or $3 a week. Every little bit adds up.

January 23

Your body is a temple, so make sure to keep your temple clean and free of harmful peer pressures. You only get one temple in life, so take care of it now. Once it's gone, it's gone.

January 24

Today is a good day to start a journal. Writing down your thoughts and emotions helps free your brain of all the weight and opens up space for new creativity.

January 25

Give a big hug to the woman in your life who is always there for you. It could be your mother, grandmother, aunt, sister, cousin, or teacher. It isn't easy raising a teenage girl.

January 26

Be a motivator in your community; start a neighborhood can drive, or a clothing drive. It feels good to give back, and it also looks great on a resume.

January 27

When you go to bed tonight; tell God thank you. He's been better to you than you could ever be to yourself. Even when you probably didn't deserve it.

January 28

In one ear and out the other, is a very powerful method. When your haters start hating, let it go in one ear and out the other, no use in wasting valuable memory space on people who don't even matter to you.

January 29

You are what you eat. What are you? Eating healthy is a way of telling God; thank you for my temple and I will respect it. Fruits and vegetables, and clean meats are the way to go. Sugar, fats, starches will break your body down.

January 30

Hey, need some extra cash. Try babysitting, a paper route, filing for the neighborhood church, or try a department store if you are old enough. It's never too soon to enter into the wonderful world of employment. It will help you to build a great work ethic.

January 31

You've made it through the first month of the year. You have one down and eleven more to go. Just keep moving. You can't stop now. There's lots to be done.

February

February 1

Entering into the month of love, make sure that loving yourself is high priority. You owe it to yourself.

February 2

Love is kind, patient, and most importantly unselfish. When you truly love someone you go the extra mile, you make it about them and not all about you.

February 3

Love: a feeling of warm personal attachment or deep affection, as for a parent, child, or friend. Who do you love? Your family, friends? Make sure you show it.

February 4

"For God so loved the world that he gave his one and only Son, that whosoever believes in him shall not perish but have eternal life." ~John 3:16. All you have to do is believe.

February 5

Beware of the *"I love you,"* from the little boy that you can't keep your eye off of and he can't keep his eye off of you. You have plenty of time for that after college. Run as fast as you can. Don't let anything get in the way of your goals. It doesn't matter how cute he is.

February 6

Don't hold back on telling someone that you love them, no matter how many times it's been said. Love has no limit.

February 7

Love is sometimes referred to as being the *"international language"*, overriding cultural and linguistic divisions.

February 8

Having true love and confidence within, is the true meaning of a girl who is knows who she really is. And nothing will jeopardize that for her.

February 9

Your color for today is red. Let it represent your boldness in the fact that you are comfortable in your love for yourself. It can be a bright shade or a bold shade. It doesn't matter, you get the point.

February 10

Don't make a boy a priority during this time in your life; just consider him an option for the future. That is if he can still pass the test.

February 11

A person doesn't really know you until they see all the beauty that lies within you. And if they don't see it, they will never know the real you.

February 12

Having a boyfriend is not always the answer, you should use the alone time to get to know you. Figure out what it takes to make you happy.

February 13

You don't need make-up or skimpy close to get others attention. Your intelligence is far more appealing.

February 14

Happy Valentine's Day! Tell yourself how much you love you.

February 15

Your heart is more than just an organ that pumps blood throughout blood vessels. Its beat is the driving force that pushes you to a place where possibilities are endless.

February 16

Heartbreak is God's way of saying that you deserve so much more. You puts you through things with certain people so you will know how not to be treated.

February 17

Don't be a needy girl who has to have a boyfriend, but be a girl a good boyfriend needs.

February 18

Being a girl who down plays her intelligence for the attention of a boy is like slapping God in the face for supplying you with a brain. If that young man doesn't appreciate your intellect; he isn't worth your time. You will get bored anyway.

February 19

Love is a privilege, and not always a right, so never take it lightly. When someone tells you that they love you; it has a way of making your day seem so much better.

February 20

Are you a daddy's girl? If so that's okay, because daddy sometimes sets the standard of how a young man should treat you. He is also a protector and never wants to see his little girl hurt.

February 21

No always means no. If someone is pressuring you for anything, don't be afraid to tell someone. Silence can be deadly.

February 22

How you carry yourself can be a huge factor in the people you attract. If you are attracting negativity, laziness, liars, and deceivers; I would say it's time for you to make a change. Don't you agree?

February 23

Demand respect; your name is not baby, honey, or shorty. You have a name and they need to use it. Don't answer to just any old thing. It isn't becoming of a lady.

February 24

A young man should like you the way you are. Your size, hair color, or clothes should not matter at all. And if it does; tell him to take his shallow behind somewhere else. He isn't worthy of your time.

February 25

A parent's love for their child is unconditional no matter the mess ups. Remember to tell them how much you love them in return. Your parents are building blocks that help you reach your goals.

February 26

Yes Jesus loves you for the bible tells you so. You should read the bible more often. It's like putting together the pieces of the puzzle of life. You won't feel so lost.

February 27

Love is in the air simply because you're you. Love doesn't require special attributes. You being the best person you can be is all that's required.

February 28

Do you know the love of a grandmother? It's so warm and comforting. It's a love that sticks with you through life and generation after generation. After all, didn't she teach your parents to love? If you know that love, never forget it, because it bridges gaps.

February 29

It's Leap Year. Get ready to leap into a new month of new adventures. But don't forget to spread love as you're leaping. It's a requirement.

March

March 1

Spread you dreams as wide as wings. And just imagine how far you will soar with your feet never touching the ground.

March 2

A word to the wise; it is considered a compliment when a 50 year old-woman looks like a teenager. However it is a complaint when a teenager looks like a 50 year-old woman. Baby girl; don't try to grow up too fast.

March 3

"Our greatest glory consists not in never falling, but in rising every time we fall." ~Oliver Goldsmith

March 4

"A girl should be two things: classy and fabulous." ~ Coco Chanel

March 5

Class is knowing what to say, when to say it, and when to keep your mouth shut.

March 6

"Always bear in mind that your own resolution to succeed is more important than any other." ~ Abraham Lincoln

March 7

Remember to always stand for something or you will fall for anything, whether you believe in it or not.

March 8

Elegance is not about being noticed, it's about being remembered and often thought about. Any girl can be noticed for whatever reason, but an elegant girl stays on the mind.

March 9

Act like a young lady, think like a warrior. Don't let the soft exterior fool them, because you're tough as nails on the inside. You are no one's push over.

March 10

A positive attitude makes a young girl beautiful. A negative attitude makes a young girl bitter and annoying. Do you know this girl? She gets on your nerves doesn't she?

March 11

Never underestimate the power of a girl who knows where she's going in life. She can't be stopped, so they better hold on, or she will run them over.

March 12

Don't wait for a prince, but wait for a guy that thinks you are a princess. That is how you deserve to be treated, and settle for nothing less.

March 13

Be the girl that you'd one day want your daughter to be. Be the girl you'd one day want your son to date.

March 14

Playing dress up begins at an early age, and you should never let it end. Remember putting on your mommy's dresses and shoes; you pretended you were a queen. What's a girl without an imagination?

March 15

If you are trapped between your feelings and what other people think is right, always go for whatever makes you happy, unless you want everybody to be happy except you. That's no way to live.

March 16

In order for someone to insult you, you must first value their opinion. Opinions are like headaches; everyone has had one before and they are hard to get rid of.

March 17

Winners never quit and quitters never win. If you lose, just keep trying, because you learn something new each time and before you know it, you've conquered it.

March 18

Refuse to worry. Refuse to be defeated. Refuse to give up.

March 19

Instead of saying to yourself; *"I think I can."* Say; *"I know I can."* That attitude is going to take you far in life.

March 20

You have to learn the rules of the game. And then you have to play better than anyone else. ~ Albert Einstein

March 21

Sometimes you don't realize your own strength until you come face to face with your greatest weakness.

March 22

You are a survivor; you can handle any tough situation that comes your way. I'm that confident in you.

March 23

Always trust in yourself; you know more than you think you do, young lady. Don't rely on others to make up your mind for you.

March 24

Each second that passes is another moment to turn it all around for the better. Time is a gift not a guarantee, so don't take advantage of it.

March 25

Stop thinking about what could go wrong and start thinking of what could go right. It turns your whole outlook around and gives you something to look forward to.

March 26

"For beautiful eyes, look for the good in others; for beautiful lips, speak only words of kindness; and for poise, walk with the knowledge that you are never alone." ~ Audrey Hepburn

March 27

Life and death lies in the power of your own tongue. Please be careful what you say. You don't want your words to come back on you.

March 28

You shouldn't want to be better than everybody else; you should want to be better than you ever thought you could be.

March 29

Without God, you can do nothing. With God there is nothing you cannot do.

March 30

Acne is a teenager's worst enemy. It pops up at the wrong time and can be very unattractive. Just remember to keep your hands out of your face. The dirt on your fingers feeds those little suckers. Drink plenty of water.

March 31

Barbie has nothing on you my dear. She's cute and all, but the girl is unrealistic and plastic. You are real and fabulously made. From every freckle that may be on your face to every curve or slant to contours your body. Barbie wishes she was you.

April

April 1

There are many bright colors in all darkness that may surround you; but you have to be able to turn the lights on in the atmosphere to see it, not matter how scary it is.

April 2

You are who you are, and no one's approval is needed to be you. God made you so that you could be you. You are better at it than anyone else.

April 3

The most memorable people in life will be the friends who loved you even when you weren't very lovable.

April 4

The worst person to be around is the one who complains about everything and appreciates nothing. What are you grateful for?

April 5

In order to fly, you have to give up the things that weigh you down. Who and what is holding you back? Let it go.

April 6

In life you never lose real friends, you just find out who your real ones are. Sometimes you have to let God do the separating in your life. He doesn't people around you who will hinder you.

April 7

False Evidence Appearing Real. That is all fear is. ~ Hill Harper

Bind the spirit of fear in the name of Jesus.

April 8

What consumes your mind controls your life. Where are your thoughts? Hopefully they're on something magnificent.

April 9

Karma will definitely come back to bite you in the butt, so be careful what you sow because you will reap it. That person you were talking bad about at school? Uh huh. Ask for forgiveness.

April 10

Never chase friendships or nourish a friendship on your own. A real friend who appreciates you will always walk with you.

April 11

Little lady if something is not happening for you, it doesn't mean it's never going to happen. It just means it hasn't happened yet. It's coming, I promise.

April 12

Just when the caterpillar thought the world was over, it became a beautiful butterfly. Even the ugliest situation can turn out to beautiful.

April 13

It's spring time. My crystal ball is showing me that floral scents should be your perfume this season. As the flowers bloom so should you.

April 14

If someone is strong enough to bring you down, show them you are strong enough to get up. Don't let them see you sweat. I bet they will think twice before messing with you again.

April 15

Little sister you will never become who you want to be if you keep blaming everyone else for who you are. If there is something about you that you don't like; change it. It's that easy.

April 16

The people who know the least about you are always the ones who have the most to say. Don't prove to them that they are wrong; prove it to yourself. They aren't worth it.

April 17

It is far more important to look ahead than to look back. You can't change the past, but you can do better in the future.

April 18

Courage is going from failure to failure without losing the drive to keep trying. It's not easy, but the sense of accomplishment is worth it.

April 19

If it weren't for bad times, you wouldn't know the good times. You just have to remember there is a rainbow after the rain. Your tears are the rain and your smile is the rainbow.

April 20

The world we have created is a product of our thinking; it cannot be changed without changing our thinking.

~Albert Einstein

April 21

Believing you can, means you're already halfway there.

April 22

Today is never too late to be a brand new better you. Especially if you know you can do better. The mature step is admitting it.

April 23

Kind words can be short and easy to speak but their echoes are truly endless. ~ Mother Teresa

April 24

When you stay up late every night, I bet you realize it's a bad idea the next morning. You then start to miss those naps in pre-school. Get your rest, your body needs it.

April 25

Be the kind of girl that, when your feet hit the floor each morning, the devil says, 'Oh crap, she's up.' Run his behind over.

April 26

Remember, you're braver than you believe, stronger than you seem and smarter than you think.

April 27

Sometimes it's best to keep your plans a secret. Everyone doesn't have your best interest at heart. It's like the saying *"don't tell right hand what your left hand is doing."* It's not being deceitful and just you fool proofing you plan.

April 28

If you continually give, you will continually have. God is pleased with a cheerful giver. It doesn't have to be money; it can be your time and commitment.

April 29

Shoot for moon. Even if you miss it you will land among the stars.

~Les Brown

April 30

Have you done your good deed for the week? Good deeds = blessings. Pump an elderly person's gas, hold the door open for someone, or even give a friend in need a hug.

May

May 1

Your happiness is intertwined with your outlook on life. Stay positive. It will take you further and further. If an opportunity doesn't present itself; create one.

May 2

Remember your body is a temple, no one should touch it other than your husband and I know you're not married. Get the point?

May 3

Do not mistake temptation for opportunity. Temptation is short lived and usually comes with regrets. An opportunity is lasting and fruitful in its return.

May 4

You are young, gifted and attractive. There is nothing you can't do you if put your mind and heart to.

May 5

Why don't you suggest movie night with your family? Time spent with family is a cherished moment and you will miss it when you are away at college; no matter how much you want to deny it.

May 6

You have an intriguing piece of equipment for success; it's called a brain, use it properly. Don't let it get corrupted with junk and viruses.

May 7

What activities are you involved in at school? It feels good to be involved in something that gets your voice heard.

May 8

Grand adventures await you if you are willing to turn the next corner. You can't stay in one place forever, or you will never go anywhere.

May 9

All your hard work and dedication is going to pay off. When it happens remember this day and that I told you so.

May 10

Pat yourself on the back for creating an opportunity. You have to encourage yourself as well as reward yourself. It is not in vain.

May 11

A liar is not believed even though she tells many truths. Honesty is the best policy, just remember the boy who cried wolf.

May 12

Success comes from diligence and not giving up on your dreams no matter how hard the journey has been.

May 13

If you feel like you don't have anyone to talk to; talk to God, He always listens baby girl. And you don't even have to text him.

May 14

If you want the sunshine, you must put up with the rain. Rain doesn't last always.

May 15

They say that in youth and beauty, wisdom is rare. Prove them wrong. You're not the average girl, you are so much more.

May 16

Good sense is the master of human life. It keeps you out of trouble and helps you to make better decisions.

May 17

When you are a true believer and know that God will take care of you; all your worries are over. No matter the situation.

May 18

New clothes don't make the girl; the girl definitely makes the clothes. A real little diva knows how to rock her old clothes just as good as she rocks the new ones.

May 19

Ignorance never settles a question. Learn to research before you answer, even though you think you know everything at this age.

May 20

Try to have a potential urge and ability for accomplishment. Don't be a girl who never finishes what she starts. It's not a good trait.

May 21

To your parents you will always be their baby. They don't mean any harm; they just want to protect you. Thank God for them no matter how much they get on your nerves.

May 22

None of the secrets of success will work unless you do. Homework maybe annoying now, but it's equipping you for success in future. Knowledge is the key.

May 23

You can always find happiness in a place where you are loved. There's no place like home. There's no place like home. There's no place like home.

May 24

The first step to better times is to imagine them. *"You got to see it before you see it or you never will see it."*

May 25

Face facts with dignity. You have to accept the things that you cannot change. There's nothing you can do about it anyway. So find the good out of every situation.

May 26

Avert misunderstandings by being calm, poised, and balanced. It's not worth getting yourself riled up. And you don't have to be angry and scream to get your point across.

May 27

You will be fortunate in everything you put your hands on. You just have to believe that.

May 28

Try to remember all your love ones who have passed away this Memorial Day weekend. They are gone but never forgotten.

May 29

Lady Bug you are free to invent your life, just make sure the invention is something you want to live with 50 years down the road.

May 30

Trust your intuition baby girl; it's God's way of giving you an answer to a problem or question. It may not be the answer you wanted, but you got it.

May 31

Simplicity and clarity should be your theme when you're communicating with others; there is no need to give someone the wrong impression. Being able to articulate yourself is a great tool.

June

June 1

The days you work on preparing your future are the best days. It's considered the ground breaking ceremony.

June 2

The secret of getting ahead is getting started. The rest can be a cake walk. Notice I said can be.

June 3

Your endurance and persistence will be rewarded with favor and success. It's inevitable.

June 4

The time is right for you to make new friends. Find friends that you can learn great things from. You never know who you may have to teach one day.

June 5

God will give you the desires of your heart if you seek him and ask for it. It seems pretty simple to me.

June 6

Can I tell you a secret; your smile will tell you what makes you happy. Keep Smiling.

June 7

When someone tells you that your dream is stupid; they're just jealous because they don't know how to dream themselves. Or they're just mad because they didn't think of it.

June 8

Now is a good time to start thinking about what college you want to attend. Research the college registration requirements and offerings. I guarantee, you will be steps ahead of the others.

June 9

As you get older, learn to prepare for the unexpected. Life is a little easier when you have an immediate solution to a problem.

June 10

While the summer is here, I know it's hot, but be careful in your clothing choices. You don't want to reveal too much. On your weeding day you want to be able to show your husband a gift that no one has ever seen.

June 11

A warm smile is a testimony of a generous and kind nature. It shows that the person appreciates life, and will go the extra mile to brighten someone's day.

June 12

Your heart will always make itself known through your words. It's something that is hard to cover up. It's deeply rooted.

June 13

Count your blessings by thinking of those who have always supported you. Never take them for granted.

June 14

Sometimes little and often makes much. A little bit everyday goes a long way. A shirt here and a pant there will one day be a wardrobe.

June 15

The day always seems prosperous to those who remain cheerful and optimistic. They always see the bright side.

June 16

School pressures will eventually fade and joy will take their place. You need to be patient and know that it's just a prayer away and high school only lasts four years.

June 17

Speaking honestly and openly, guarantees that your voice will be heard. Speaking lies will guarantee that no one will listen to you. They won't believe you anyway.

June 18

The scars don't matter. Who is without a flaw? No one I tell you, no one.

June 19

There are times when it is much wiser to take advice than to give it. Constructive criticism can be very helpful when it's coming from the right person.

June 20

Many false steps in life are made standing still because you are too afraid that people will laugh at your dreams.

June 21

The skills you have gathered while being a teen will one day come in handy when you're a grown woman.

June 22

You were born with five senses and sometimes it better to use one more than the others. It can be better to listen than to talk.

June 23

It should not be about the competition in the game, it should be about the preparation for the sport. Did you put in the time and effort to secure the win?

June 24

There are always three sides to every story; your side, the other person's side, and the truth. Stick to the truth and you will surely win the battle.

June 25

To be able to practice five things everywhere under heaven constitutes perfect virtue... gravity, generosity of soul, sincerity, earnestness, and kindness. ~ Confucius

June 26

Pray for what you need, and work for the things you want. God won't do anything for you that you can do for yourself. Let's not be lazy.

June 27

As your purse is filled to capacity of all the things that makes a girl smile, make sure your heart is filled as well.

June 28

Children, obey your parents in everything, for this pleases the Lord. Colossians 3:20

June 29

Laughing at someone because they don't have what you have, say's a few things about you. It says that you're conceited, shallow, and downright mean. Please don't be that girl.

June 30

Smiling often can make you look and feel younger. I know it will at least keep the wrinkles away for now.

July

July 1

There should always be a true and sincere friendship between you and your friends. The same way you trust them, is the same way they should be able to trust you.

July 2

Fame and riches are not the true meaning of success; the true meaning is you being happy in life without them.

July 3

Don't let anyone look down on you because you are young, but set an example for the believers in speech, in life, in love, in faith and in purity. 1Timothy 4:12

July 4

As you celebrate independence today, think of all the men who fought hard and those who lost their lives so that you can be free.

July 5

You can find beauty in ordinary things; it's just a matter of looking at something on the inside. Beauty is inside out, not outside in.

July 6

It is less painful to learn in youth than to be ignorant in age. ~ Proverb

July 7

Never hide your talents, showcase them for the world to see. You never know who is watching. Your big break could be right around the corner.

July 8

Anger begins with folly, and ends with regret. It's not worth it, and at the end of the day you will probably forget what you were angry at in the first place.

July 9

A blessing can come from anyone, so don't be so quick to turn your nose at others. Even a homeless person can speak a word in your life that will show you what's needed to keep you from being homeless.

July 10

Wear fruity lip gloss this summer. A little shimmer has never hurt anybody. And it smells and taste pretty darn good.

July 11

Youth is the best time to be rich, and the best time to be poor.

~ Euripides.

July 12

When you look at your window at night, wish on as many stars as you can see. Wishes do come true. Continue to be the little girl that believes in miracles.

July 13

Your greatest fortune is not the number of friends you have, but if you have one true friend. One friend is better than five fake ones.

July 14

Honor your father and your mother, so that you may live long in the land the Lord your God is giving you. ~ Exodus 20:12

July 15

If you are a young lady with curves; consider those curves a protective device that bounces you back on your feet when someone has knocked you down mentally or physically.

July 16

The joyfulness of a young woman will prolong her days. When you are genuinely joyful, you can't wait to see what the next day's joy bring.

July 17

It takes more than one good memory to have good memories. Start creating memorable moments today and never forget them.

July 18

Always look for new outlets to express your creative abilities. Maybe join an art circle, even a book club, or made take sewing lessons.

July 19

There's no substitute for hard work. ~ Thomas Edison.

July 20

A good friend is a present you give yourself. But you must be one in return.

July 21

Just living is not enough. One must have sunshine, freedom, and a little flower. ~ Hans Christian Anderson

July 22

The beginning of wisdom is simply to desire it. If you want it bad enough, I'm sure you will get it.

July 23

Please and thank you are the easiest forms of gratitude. Not too hard right?

July 24

Let there be magic in your smile and firmness in your handshake. Let them know you didn't come to play.

July 25

I see you in yellow today. Let the brightness shine as bright as your bubbly personality.

July 26

Whatever storm you are going through is almost gone. Can you see the sun peeking through the clouds? It will be over soon.

July 27

Strong and bitter words indicate a weak soul that doesn't know how to convey how they really feel.

July 28

Doesn't it feel good when people say good things about you? Keep them talking.

July 29

A single kind word will keep one warm for years.

July 30

When you pray today, ask God for life, health, and strength. You can't make it without them.

July 31

The good will always out way the bad, just wait and see. It doesn't look like it at the moment, but it will.

August

August 1

Success is a journey, not a destination. ~ Satenig St. Marie

August 2

Your heart is a place to draw true happiness and peace, so don't just give it to any old body.

August 3

Be nice to people on your way up. You may meet them on your way down.

August 4

Give the world the best you have and the best will come back to you. It called good karma.

August 5

Do not let society paralyze you with its limits. Break free from the constraints.

August 6

God can do wonders with a broken heart if we give him all the pieces to put it back together.

August 7

Each day comes just once in a life time; today you are creating tomorrow's past.

August 8

If the idea you had five days ago still looks good, do it. It's hanging on your minds sub conscience for a reason.

August 9

Communication is your most important source of power.

August 10

A true friend asks only for your time, not your money or things. Beware of the manipulator, because they are out there.

August 11

In the cookies of life, parents are considered the chocolate chips. They are there in every bite. Even in the bad bites they will be there for you.

August 12

Before you make an important decision, please seek counsel first. You don't want any regrets later.

August 13

Always keep your face toward the sunshine, and the shadows will fall behind you. And you will never know that they exist.

August 14

Are you still writing in your journal? I hope so. Remember you have to release to make room for more.

August 15

If life were a blank canvas, what would you choose to paint on it? Would you use bold colors or pastels? Would you have fine lines or broad-wide strokes?

August 16

Are you taking your vitamins? Vitamins provide supplements that you may not be getting in some foods you eat. It also gives you the energy you need to conquer the world.

August 17

To keep the brain sharp, you must keep feeding it. Read. Read. Read.

August 18

"There is only one pretty child in the world, and every mother has it."

~ Chinese Proverb

August 19

Crying has a way of cleansing the soul. If the tears need to fall, let them. You need to be refreshed.

August 20

The purpose of education is to turn mirrors into windows. Remember that the next time you are reluctant to pick up a book to study.

August 21

Sometimes when you win you actually lose, and sometimes when you lose, you actually win. You have to be mature enough to know which is which.

August 22

Now is the most precious time. Seize it, live it, because it shall never come again.

August 23

What music do you have on your IPod? Is it uplifting or is it degrading? Music is supposed to soothe the soul not conform and corrupt the way you think.

August 24

If you doubt that God is real; look at all the beauty that He created in nature, and within yourself. He is an awesome wonder.

August 25

I know it's hard trying to keep up with school, friends, and activities. But try doing all that with a baby. Just say no. You are not ready sweetie.

August 26

Take pride in everything you do. If it's something that you aren't proud of, then you shouldn't be doing it.

August 27

Right now it may seem like you are a little girl in a big world. But later it will seem like you're a big girl in a wonderful world of opportunities.

August 28

What goes around comes around. Don't dish it if you can't take it, because it's definitely coming back.

August 29

The happiest people in life are not those getting more, but those giving more.

August 30

All problems are blessings given to us to learn from.

August 31

Make sure you get a least thirty minutes of exercise this week. Healthy is the new fabulous. Didn't you know?

September

September 1

C's are ok on a report card but A's and B's are so much better. Don't settle for average.

September 2

A clean conscience is a soft pillow. It makes it easy to sleep at night when you don't have the burden of guilt on your heart.

September 3

The smart thing in life to do is be you. You are better at it than anyone else in the whole world.

September 4

Being the center of attention is not always a bad thing; but it depends on the kind of attention you are receiving.

September 5

If he really loves you like he says he does, then he will wait for you. If doesn't wait he doesn't really love you.

September 6

After graduation, you enter upon the time of life where you are responsible for grading your own answers. You are now held accountable for your own work.

September 7

The social scene of being popular can be fun today, but can be devastating tomorrow. Choose your fun wisely.

September 8

A family that prays together stays together. Prayer builds a bond that can't be broken by life's misfortunes.

September 9

People tend to get what they expect. So expect the best and that's exactly what you will get.

September 10

Keep your heart pure, your mind clear, and your soul innocent.

September 11

Find your passion. When you love what you do it's not considered work. Now you know the secret.

September 12

Don't ever be afraid to speak up for yourself. You owe it to yourself.

September 13

How to save money 101; If the option is between buying a new pair of shoes or buying food, toiletries, or school supplies; please choose the latter. It's nothing like having a new pair of shoes and a growling stomach. It's not cute.

September 14

Life is full of tests. God will continue to put you in the same situation over and over again until the one day the light bulb turns on and you say *"I've got it."* In order to go to the next level you have to past the test.

September 15

On the days when Mother Nature has you regretting your femininity, just bear it and take a couple of Midol. It only lasts five days. LOL.

September 16

A good friend is someone who will listen to your problems. A great friend is someone who will sit up all night with you to help you find a solution to the problems.

September 17

Try to be better than you were yesterday, and tomorrow be better than you are today.

September 18

Poor is a state of mind. If you think poor you will be poor. If you think rich you will be rich, even if you only have a dollar in your pocket. You won't stay that way.

September 19

What do you call a pretty, educated, successful, and happy woman? Answer: you in just a few short years.

September 20

Do not rush through life, take a minute and enjoy it. Once the days are gone sweetheart, you can never get them back.

September 21

Makeup tip for the day: Less is more. Let your natural beauty shine.

September 22

Have you ever been in a situation where you said something but later thought of something better to say? Just be patient I'm sure the opportunity will present its self again.

September 23

A true teen diva never falls for the cheesy pickup lines. She knows that she is worth more than that and doesn't mind telling him so.

September 24

This is the day that the Lord has made. Rejoice and be glad in it.

September 25

Wear your hair down today and let the tresses blow in the wind, wild and carefree.

September 26

It doesn't matter if you are a cheerleader chick or a tomboy; just whatever you are, be good at it.

September 27

Are you involved in your church? If not, get active fast, because an idle mind is the devils playground.

September 28

Does your family sit together at the table for dinner? If not suggest it and initiate the conversation. A simple *"how was your day,"* can bring a family closer together.

September 29

If you have a little sister or brother; remember they are watching everything you do. Set a standard that they can follow proudly. No pressure.

September 30

Do something unusual tomorrow. Sometimes the normal routine needs a change of scenery.

October

October 1

The world doesn't always wear a friendly face. You just have to learn to have thick skin, roll with the punches, and don't take it personal.

October 2

Life seems to begin at the age of thirteen. You finally have the word *"teen"* in your age and now you get to sit at the big table during the holidays.

October 3

If you have people messing with you, ask Jesus to be a fence. That way you will have protection all around you.

October 4

Your personality is a glass that should always be filled and never drained. Keep pouring into it.

October 5

Each day comes bearing gifts; even if it's just the gift of life itself.

October 6

In order for you not to have bags and worry lines by the time you're twenty, you must learn to stop worrying and give it to the Lord.

October 7

Beyoncé's *"Who Rule the World,"* song just may be the tune to help motivate you to climb the mole hill that seems like a mountain.

October 8

When seeking advice from others, it is always a good idea to analyze their credibility. The blind should never lead the blind.

October 9

If something sounds too good to be true, it probably is, but don't be too quick to shrug it off. Learn the facts first.

October 10

By the time you turn sixteen, you should start working on a resume. If you've never had a job before, just add all your school activities or volunteer work. If you don't volunteer now is a good time to start.

October 11

What does your nail polish say about you? Pink: sweet, blue: carefree, purple: precious, red: fun, yellow: innocent, or black: confident.

October 12

Take the time to study a few great women before you; i.e. Harriet Tubman, Eleanor Roosevelt, Ellen Ochoa, and Empress Wu Zetian. These women paved the way for you young ladies today.

October 13

Make sure you moisturize your skin every day. The key to having flawless skin when you're older is to protect it while you're young.

October 14

Beware of boys bearing gifts. And ask yourself the questions; *"what does he want in return?"* It better be nothing.

October 15

A lie is something that you will easily forget, but the truth will always be remembered. Tell the truth and then you won't ever get caught in a lie.

October 16

Think before you speak; you never want to intentionally hurt someone's feelings.

October 17

Never give just to receive. When you give from the heart you are blessed times two.

October 18

Every girl needs to learn a specialty dish, and not just cereal and milk. Spaghetti is a good start. It's quick and easy.

October 19

The simplest times in your life can be the fun times in your life. Who doesn't love balling up on the couch with a bowl of ice cream watching their favorite movie?

October 20

Behind every fascinating teen girl......is a drawer full of nail polish, make-up, and hair brushes. There is nothing wrong with being prissy.

October 21

Have you had your first heart break? Don't worry because five years down the road you're going to say to yourself *what was I thinking?*

October 22

Body odor is a very bad first impression. No one wants to be remembered as the stinky girl.

October 23

Are you a girl with caviar taste with cheeseburger money? Don't feel bad, we have all been there.

October 24

Do you aspire to be an actress or model when you grow up? That's great; just don't forget about careers like teaching and nursing.

October 25

Learn to be patient with the older generation. That's going to be you one day.

October 26

An unhappy woman was once an unhappy girl. Fix it now. Don't carry the junk into your future. Find what makes you happy.

October 27

A smart girl plans for the week on the weekend, so her week days will be stress free.

October 28

Your body is beginning to go through different changes. If you have any questions ask a responsible adult like your mom, nurse, or counselor. Don't get wrong information from your peers. They know about as much as you do or maybe even less.

October 29

You know how you say that you can't wait to get out of school so you won't have to deal with teachers anymore. Well guess what? You're going to have a boss someday and they are going to do the same thing your teacher did; tell you what to do.

October 30

Are you counting calories? If so that's ok. Just know you don't have to be a size two to be beautiful. Do it for your health, not your weight.

October 31

Beware of goblins and goons. Whatever your plans are, be safe for Halloween. Stay with a group, don't wear a costume that sends the wrong message, and make sure you check all your candy if you still go trick-or-treating.

November

November 1

Don't be easily influenced by everybody. You, my little sister must learn who you can and cannot trust.

November 2

We are often told that the best things in life are free; but sometimes you get what you pay for.

November 3

Please stop putting all your business on Facebook. There are just some things that people do not need to know about you. ;-)

November 4

A girl's emergency kit consists of; toothbrush, toothpaste, tampons or pads, deodorant, a clean pair of undies, a brush, and a mirror. It saves lives. LOL.

November 5

Say it loud *"I'm a girl and I'm Proud."* Say it loud *"I'm a girl and I'm Proud."*

November 6

Try to keep your camera handy, so that you can capture the moments that will one day be forgotten.

November 7

Don't confuse fashion with hoochie. Fashion is an ensemble that adorns the body gracefully. Hoochie is any old tired outfit that shows too much skin. See the difference.

November 8

Every time you reach one goal, set another one. It's an ongoing process that keeps you from getting complacent.

November 9

Learning to speak publicly is a great skill to have. All powerful people have to do this at least once in their life. Learn now.

November 10

Passing judgment on others is not fair and, is not your job. You never know what a person has gone through in life, just like they don't know what you have gone through.

November 11

Don't act on emotion. Take time to calm down and act with a clear head. You will thank me later.

November 12

When people are unhappy with themselves, they will try to find fault in everything you do. Pray for them and keep it moving.

November 13

Thankful: feeling or expressing gratitude; appreciative.

November 14

Live for today, learn from yesterday's mistake, and look to tomorrow's promises.

November 15

Look for the good in everyone, it just may out way the bad.

November 16

Beauty can be found in the most uncommon places. The dark and dampest surfaces can blossom the most beautiful flowers.

November 17

There are three things to having gorgeous hair; conditioner, conditioner, and more conditioner. It's the cure for split ends.

November 18

If you speak happiness, you will have it. If you speak misfortune you will receive it.

November 19

Gossip is started by people who have nothing else better to do with their time. That sounds pretty pathetic to me.

November 20

The Lord's Prayer: Our Father which art in heaven, Hallowed be thy name. Thy kingdom come, Thy will be done in earth, as it is in heaven. Give us this day our daily bread. And forgive us our debts, as we forgive our debtors. And lead us not into temptation, but deliver us from evil: For thine is the kingdom, and the power, and the glory, forever. Amen. ~ Matthew 6:9-13

November 21

A selfish person's acts are done with an agenda of some form of return. An unselfish person's acts are done with no desire of return, just to provide help.

November 22

Younger siblings are your greatest cheerleaders for success; because they can't wait for you to go to college so they can get the bigger room.

November 23

"We can't solve problems by using the same kind of thinking we used when we created them." ~ Albert Einstein

November 24

Indulge a little on Thanksgiving Day. Don't worry about the calories; just make sure you hit a hard workout on Monday.

November 25

What are you thankful for this Thanksgiving? Whatever it is, show appreciation for it.

November 26

Learn to be happy of other's success. There is enough to go around for everybody. Yours is on the way.

November 27

A mother's hug has a way of making all the bad go away. On the bad days tell mommy you need a hug. It will make you feel so much better.

November 28

The wise man, even when he holds his tongue, says more than the fool when he speaks. ~ Yiddish Proverb

November 29

And the LORD answered me, and said, write the vision, and make it plain upon tables, that he may run that readeth it. ~ Habakkuk 2:2.

Keep journaling.

November 30

When people leave your company; make sure they leave with an awesome last impression of you.

December

December 1

Don't you just love the month of December? It's the time for families to join together and be at peace. What is your contribution to the peacefulness this year?

December 2

Tomorrow is not promised to anyone. So make all amends today and always tell the people you love, how you feel.

December 3

Dress for the season and not the weather. Bundle up and take vitamin C. Prevention is the best way to treat a cold.

December 4

I see a tree trimming party bringing your family and friends closer together.

December 5

Famous words of my grandfather; *"If you don't have three times the amount in your bank account; don't put it on your credit card."* That's a great lesson right there.

December 6

"Bah Humbug" No one wants to be around a scrooge during the holidays. Cheer up, I promise you it's not as bad as you think.

December 7

Learn to talk to God during the good times, not just the bad.

December 8

I'm wishing your holiday season be filled with cheer, family, and great fortune.

December 9

Experience is a good teacher, but don't go through the rough stuff if you don't have to.

December 10

Don't let the joy of Christmas be measured by the amount of money that is spent on the gift. There is someone out there who is just wishing for a hot meal this Christmas.

December 11

Do something special for dad this year. He was the one who chased all the monsters from under your bed.

December 12

The best holiday present is a warm welcome to family and friends.

December 13

Be careful not to burn your bridge; you never know when you might have to walk back across it.

December 14

Start new family traditions this season and keep them going for years to come.

December 15

Having a younger sister means having a lock on your door, or you will see her in your clothes without your permission.

December 16

If you are low on cash or don't have any at all this Christmas, how about you make gifts this year? Get those creative juices flowing.

December 17

I see you in earmuffs today. They can be a great accessory, and it will keep Jack Frost from nipping at your ears.

December 18

Santa Claus is coming to town. Have you been naughty or nice? Hopefully you have been nice.

December 19

If you don't have a fire place to warm your chills; a cup of hot chocolate will do the trick.

December 20

Treat every day as if it's Christmas by giving the gift of your smile.

December 21

Have a holly jolly Christmas. Turn up the carols, warm up the apple cider, and let the good times roll.

December 22

Today is a good day for you to sign your family up to volunteer at a local homeless shelter or soup kitchen this holiday. It will make you realize how blessed you really are.

December 23

Holiday parties can be the best; you just make sure you stay away from the eggnog.

December 24

What is your gift to yourself this year? How about self-improvement?

December 25

Merry Christmas! Happy Hanukkah! Feliz Navidad! Happy Kwanza! Celebrate the true meaning this season. It's not about the gifts. It's about family and the birth of Jesus.

December 26

If you didn't get the one thing that you wanted the most for Christmas, and you're not mad about it; it means you are maturing. Good Job.

December 27

Ask God for an unveiling, so that you can tap into your purpose and do a new thing.

December 28

I hope you're enjoying the holiday vacation from school. Before you know it will be time to go back.

December 29

Are you tired of the Christmas leftovers yet? If so use the ham and turkey for sandwiches. It gives it a different spin to your taste buds.

December 30

As the year comes to a close, look over the past 12 months. If you have any regrets, try to fix them before January 1st. If you don't have enough time to fix them now, make them a priority next year.

December 31

What is your New Year's resolution? Make it count. 10..9..8..7..6..5..4..3..2..1

HAPPY NEW YEAR!!!!!!!!!

CPSIA information can be obtained at www.ICGtesting.com
Printed in the USA
BVOW03s1850280514

354762BV00011B/217/P